E-COMMERCE
SUCCESS
THE ULTIMATE
BEGINNER'S GUIDE

Styla Digital

CONTENTS

INTRODUCTION

Welcome to E-commerce Success Made Simple!

Congratulations on embarking on the exciting journey of creating your own flourishing online store! Our comprehensive e-book, "E-commerce Success: The Ultimate Beginner's Guide," stands as a valuable resource, ready to be your guide in navigating the intricate world of e-commerce. This insightful manual not only imparts essential knowledge but also equips you with practical tips, empowering you to transform your entrepreneurial dreams into a thriving reality.

Prepare to conquer the dynamic landscape of online business with unwavering confidence! This guide goes beyond the basics, providing you with a nuanced understanding of the intricacies that define success in the digital marketplace. So, gear up for an enlightening exploration into the secrets of e-commerce, and get ready to make your mark with assurance and finesse!

What to Expect from this Ebook

In this comprehensive guide, we will provide a clear breakdown of every aspect involved in starting and running an online store.

We will explain the fundamentals and help you select the most suitable tools for your needs. Our aim is to simplify and make e-commerce success easily attainable for you.

Let's get started!

HOW UNDERSTAND A TARGET MARKET, ANALYZE COMPETITORS, AND UNCOVER POTENTIAL OPPORTUNITIES FOR AN ONLINE STORE

To understand a target market, you need to research their needs, wants, and behaviors. You can do this by conducting surveys, interviews, and focus groups. You can also look at secondary data, such as census data and industry reports. Once you have a good understanding of your target market, you can start to develop marketing strategies that will appeal to them.

To analyze competitors, you need to identify who your competitors are and what they are doing well. You can do this by looking at their websites, social media pages, and marketing materials. You can also read reviews and articles about them. Once you know who your competitors are and what they are doing, you can start to develop strategies that will help you differentiate your business from theirs.

To uncover potential opportunities, you need to think about what your target market needs and wants that are not currently being met. You can do this by brainstorming, conducting surveys, and talking to your target market. Once you have identified some potential opportunities, you can start to develop strategies to capitalize on them.

Here are some additional tips for understanding your target market, analyzing competitors, and uncovering potential opportunities:

Use data to your advantage. There is a wealth of data available online that can help you understand your target market and your competitors. Use this data to inform your decision-making.

Be creative. Don't be afraid to think outside the box when it comes to understanding your target market, analyzing competitors, and uncovering potential opportunities. The best ideas often come from unexpected places.

Be persistent. It takes time and effort to understand your target market, analyze competitors, and uncover potential opportunities. Don't give up if you don't see results immediately. Keep at it, and you will eventually find success.

Here is a list of online resources that can help you understand your target market, analyze competitors, and uncover potential opportunities:

Google Trends: Google Trends is a free tool that allows you to track the popularity of search terms over time. You can use Google Trends to see how often people are searching for products or services related to your business.

Google Keyword Planner: Google Keyword Planner is a free tool that helps you find the right keywords to target in your marketing campaigns. You can use Google Keyword Planner to see how often people are searching for keywords related to your business and how competitive those keywords are.

Google Analytics: Google Analytics is a free tool that tracks website traffic. You can use Google Analytics to see how many people are visiting your website, where they are coming from, and what pages they are viewing.

Social Media Insights: Most social media platforms provide insights into your audience and how they are engaging with your content. You can use this information to understand your target market and what they are interested in.

SurveyMonkey: SurveyMonkey is a free tool that allows you to create and distribute surveys. You can use surveys to gather feedback from your target market about their needs, wants, and behaviors.

Interviews: Interviews are a great way to get in-depth feedback from your target market. You can conduct interviews in person, over the phone, or online.

Focus Groups: Focus groups are a type of interview where you gather a group of people together to discuss a specific topic. Focus groups can be a great way to get feedback on new products or services.

Industry Reports: Industry reports provide valuable information about your industry, including market size, trends, and competition. You can find industry reports online or from trade associations.

Census Data: Census data provides demographic information about the population, including age, gender, race, and income. You can use census data to understand your target market and where they live.

There are also a lot of paid services online for any need, you can access them just with a quick research in your best-loved search engine.

CREATING YOUR ONLINE PRESENCE

Choosing the Right Domain Name

Selecting the perfect domain name is crucial for your online identity.
We'll guide you through the process, offering tips and tricks to ensure you make the right choice.

The Basics of Website Design for Beginners

No need for a computer science degree! Learn the basics of website design, focusing on simplicity, user experience, and showcasing your products effectively.

Easy-to-Use Platforms for Your Online Store

Explore user-friendly platforms that simplify the process of setting up your online store. We'll highlight popular options, breaking down their features to help you make an informed decision.

BUILDING ONLINE PRESENCE FROM 0 TO A FULL WORKING WEBSITE

The first step is choose the right domain name.

Choosing the right domain name is one of the most important decisions you'll make when starting a website. A good domain name will be memorable, relevant to your business, and available. Here are a few tips on how to find the right domain name:

1. Do your research. Before you start brainstorming domain names, take some time to research your competition. What are other businesses in your industry using for their domain names? What do you like and dislike about them? Once you have a good understanding of the competition, you can start to develop a list of potential domain names for your own business.

2. Keep it short and simple. A good domain name should be easy to remember and type. Avoid using long, complex domain names that are difficult to spell or pronounce.

3. Make it relevant. Your domain name should be relevant to your business and what you offer. This will help people find your website when they're searching for information online.

4. Make it available. Once you've found a domain name that you love, make sure it's available before you register it. You can use a domain name search engine to check availability.

5. Be creative. Don't be afraid to get creative with your domain name. A unique domain name can help you stand out from the competition.

6. Use keywords. If you want your website to rank well in search engine results pages (SERPs), you should use keywords in your

domain name. This will help people find your website when they're searching for information online.

7. Avoid hyphens. Hyphens can make your domain name look unprofessional and difficult to remember. Avoid using them if possible.

8. Use .com. The .com domain extension is the most popular and well-known domain extension. If possible, you should register a .com domain for your website.

9. Use a domain name registrar. A domain name registrar is a company that sells and registers domain names. You can use a domain name registrar to register your domain name and manage your DNS settings.

10. Keep your domain name up-to-date. Make sure to keep your domain name up-to-date and renew it before it expires. This will ensure that your website remains accessible to your visitors.

Following these tips will help you find the right domain name for your business. With a little bit of research and creativity, you can find a domain name that is memorable, relevant, and available.

Next step is, now, to design your website.

Website design is the process of creating a website that is both visually appealing and easy to use. It involves a number of different elements, including the layout, the design of the pages, the use of images and text, and the overall functionality of the website.

If you are a beginner, there are a few things you can do to get started with website design. First, you need to decide what kind of website you want to create. Are you looking to create a personal website, a business website, or a blog? Once you know what kind of website you want to create, you can start to brainstorm ideas for the layout and design.

There are a number of different website design software programs that you can use to create your website. Some popular options include Adobe Dreamweaver, Wix, and Squarespace. These programs make it easy to create a website without any prior coding experience.

Once you have chosen a website design software program, you can start to create the layout of your website. The layout is the overall structure of your website. It includes the placement of the different elements on your website, such as the header, the navigation bar, the main content area, and the footer.

The design of your website is the look and feel of your website. It includes the choice of colors, fonts, and images. You want to create a design that is both visually appealing and easy to use.

Once you have created the layout and design of your website, you can start to add content. The content is the information that you want to share with your visitors. This could include text, images, videos, and links to other websites.

Finally, you need to test your website to make sure that it works properly. You should test it on different browsers and devices to make sure that it looks and works the same on all platforms.

Following these tips will help you create a website that is both visually appealing and easy to use. With a little bit of time and effort, you can create a website that will help you achieve your goals.

Here are some additional tips for website design:

Use high-quality images. Images are a great way to add visual interest to your website and make it more engaging for your visitors. Make sure to use high-quality images that are relevant to your content.

Use clear and concise text. Your text should be easy to read and understand. Avoid using jargon or technical language that your visitors may not understand.

Use a simple navigation bar. Your navigation bar should be easy to use and navigate. It should include all of the main pages on your website so that your visitors can easily find what they are looking for.

Make sure your website is mobile-friendly. More and more people are using their mobile devices to access the internet. Make sure your website is designed to be viewed on mobile devices so that your visitors can easily access your content.

Test your website regularly. Make sure to test your website regularly to make sure that it is working properly. You should test it on different browsers and devices to make sure that it looks and works the same on all platforms.

In summary, website design is a complex process that involves a number of different elements. By following these tips , you can create a website that is both visually appealing and easy to use.

But if your goal is to build an online-store...When choosing an e-commerce platform, it is important to consider your needs and budget. Some platforms are more expensive than others, but they may offer more features and customization options. It is also important to choose a platform that is easy to use and that offers good customer support.

Here are some tips for building an online store:

Choose the right e-commerce platform. There are a number of different platforms to choose from, so it is important to choose one that is right for your needs
.

Design a user-friendly website. Your website should be easy to navigate and use. Make sure to include clear and concise product descriptions and images.

Offer a variety of payment options. Your customers should be able to pay for their purchases in a variety of ways, including credit cards, PayPal, and bank transfers.

Here are some easy-to-use platforms to build an online store:

Shopify: A popular e-commerce platform that offers a wide range of features and tools. It is easy to use and can be customized to match your brand. Shopify also offers a variety of payment options and shipping options.

WooCommerce: A free WordPress plugin that can be used to create an e- commerce store. It is highly customizable and offers a variety of features, including product management, payment processing, and shipping.

Wix: A website builder that also offers an e-commerce platform. It is easy to use and offers a variety of templates and features. Wix also offers a free plan, which is a good option for businesses that are just starting out.

Squarespace: A website builder that offers an e-commerce platform. It is easy to use and offers a variety of templates and features. Squarespace also offers a free trial, which is a good option for businesses that are just starting out.

BigCommerce: A cloud-based e-commerce platform that offers a wide range of features and tools. It is easy to use and can be customized to match your brand. BigCommerce also offers a variety of payment options and shipping options.

Magento: An open-source e-commerce platform that offers a wide range of features and tools. It is highly customizable and can be used to create a large and complex online store. Magento also offers a variety of payment options and shipping options.

STARTING AND RUNNING YOUR ONLINE STORE

Simplified Steps to List Your Products

Listing your products online can be straightforward. We'll guide you through
the process of creating compelling product listings that attract customers and drive sales.

Navigating the Basics of Online Payments

Understanding online payments is essential for any e-commerce business. We'll break down the basics of payment gateways, helping you choose secure and reliable options for your customers

Tips for Efficient Order Fulfillment

Efficient order fulfillment is the key to customer satisfaction. Discover tips and tools that make managing orders and shipping a breeze, ensuring a positive experience for your buyers

STARTING AND RUNNING A STORE: EVERYTHING YOU MUST KNOW

Here are the steps on how to create compelling listings that attract customers and drive sales:

1. Choose the right product images. Your product images are the first thing potential customers will see, so it's important to make a good impression. Use clear, well-lit images that show your products off in their best light. You can use a professional photographer or take the photos yourself. If you're taking the photos yourself, make sure to use a good camera and lighting.

2. Write clear and concise product descriptions. Your product descriptions should be easy to read and understand. Include all of the important information about your product, such as the features, benefits, and specifications. You can also include customer testimonials or reviews to help convince potential customers to buy your product.

3. Use keywords throughout your listing. When potential customers are searching for products online, they're using keywords to find what they're looking for. Make sure to include relevant keywords throughout your listing so that your product

shows up in search results. You can use a keyword research tool to help you find the right keywords to use.

4. Offer competitive prices. Customers are always looking for the best deal, so it's important to offer competitive prices on your products. If you can, offer discounts or promotions to attract even more customers. You can also compare your prices to those of your competitors to make sure you're offering a fair price.

5. Provide excellent customer service. Customers want to feel confident that they're making a good purchase, so it's important to provide excellent customer service. Be responsive to customer inquiries and make sure to resolve any issues quickly and efficiently. You can also offer a money-back guarantee or return policy to give customers peace of mind.

6. Market your listings. Once you've created compelling listings, it's important to market them so that potential customers can find them. You can do this by advertising on social media, search engines, and other channels. You can also create content that will help promote your products, such as blog posts, videos, and social media posts.

What do you need now? Of course a payment method...

A payment gateway is a system that authorizes payments for e-commerce transactions. It is a secure online payment processing system that authorizes payments for online transactions. It is a link between your online store and the bank that processes your credit card payments.

When a customer makes a purchase on your online store, they enter their credit card information into your checkout form. Your website then sends this information to the payment gateway, which authorizes the payment and sends the authorization back to your website. Your website then completes the order and sends the customer a confirmation email.

There are many different payment gateways available, and each one has its own set of features and fees. When choosing a payment gateway, you need to consider the following factors:

Security The payment gateway should be secure to protect your customers' credit card information.

Reliability: The payment gateway should be reliable so that your customers can make payments without any problems
.

Features: The payment gateway should have the features that you need, such as support for multiple payment methods.

Fees: The payment gateway should have reasonable fees so that you can keep your costs down.

Once you have chosen a payment gateway, you need to integrate it with your online store. This process will vary depending on the payment gateway and your online store platform. Once the payment gateway is integrated, you can start accepting payments from your customers.

Here are some tips for choosing a payment gateway:

Do your research. There are many different payment gateways available, so it's important to do your research and compare your options.

Read reviews. Read online reviews of different payment gateways to get an idea of what other people are saying about them.

Choose a reputable payment gateway. Make sure to choose a payment gateway that is reputable and has a good track record.

Consider your needs. When choosing a payment gateway, you need to consider your specific needs, such as the type of business you have, the payment methods you want to accept, and your budget.

Compare fees. Payment gateways typically charge fees for each transaction. Be sure to compare the fees of different payment gateways before you choose one.

Get support. Make sure to choose a payment gateway that offers good customer support in case you have any problems.

By following these tips, you can choose a payment gateway that is right for your business..

Managing orders and shipping efficiently is crucial for the success of an online store. Here are some tips and tools that can help you streamline your order management and shipping processes:

Implement analytics Utilize analytics tools to gain insights into your customers' behavior, track sales trends, and identify areas for improvement. This data can help you make informed decisions to optimize your online store's performance and customer experience.

Choose the right platform: Select an eCommerce platform that offers robust order management and shipping capabilities. Look for features like inventory management, order tracking, and integration with shipping carriers. Platforms such as Zoho Inventory, Linnworks, and Shift4Shop provide comprehensive order management solutions.

Outsource order fulfillment: Consider partnering with a dropshipping merchant or utilizing an eCommerce order fulfillment center. These services handle inventory storage, packaging, and shipping on your behalf. By outsourcing these tasks, you can save time and ensure prompt delivery to your customers.

Send abandoned cart emails: Implement abandoned cart email campaigns to encourage customers to complete their purchase. These automated emails serve as a gentle reminder and can help recover lost sales. Several apps, such as those available on the Shopify app store, can assist you in sending abandoned cart emails.

Use a helpdesk or live chat function: Provide excellent customer support by integrating a helpdesk or live chat function into your online store. This allows you to address customer queries and concerns in real-time, improving customer satisfaction and building trust. LiveAgent and Gorgias are popular helpdesk software options.

By implementing these tips and utilizing the suggested tools, you can efficiently manage your store's orders and shipping processes, leading to improved customer satisfaction and business growth. A key reminder: when selecting tools, opt for those that align seamlessly with your unique needs and overarching objectives. The right choices in this realm can be a game- changer, contributing significantly to the success and expansion of your business.

GETTING STARTED WITH E-COMMERCE

Understanding E-commerce Basics

E-commerce, or electronic commerce, is the digital realm where buying and selling goods and services take center stage. To navigate this expansive landscape effectively, it becomes paramount to grasp the fundamental principles that underpin the entire e-commerce ecosystem. Before we dive into the intricacies of its various facets, let's lay a solid foundation by comprehending the core concepts that define the world of online transactions.

Benefits of Starting an Online Store

Explore the multitude of benefits that come with establishing your very own online store. From expanding your reach to a global audience to the convenience of managing your business from any location, the advantages are endless.

Setting Realistic Goals for Success

Learn effective strategies for setting achievable goals for your online store, guaranteeing a well-defined roadmap for success. Our step-by-step approach will help you stay focused and on target throughout the goal- setting process.

MARKET RESEARCH FOR DUMMIES

Demystifying Market Research

Market research plays a vital role in guiding your e-commerce journey. Our goal is to simplify this process by helping you understand your target market, analyze your competitors, and uncover potential opportunities for your online store.

Simple Steps to Identify Your Target Audience

Discover effective strategies to define and gain a deeper understanding of your target audience. In this process, we will delve into demographics, psychographics, and behaviors to create a comprehensive profile of your ideal customers.

Tools and Resources for Easy Market Research

Market research can be simplified and made more accessible through the use of our user-friendly tools and resources. These resources will make the process of gathering information about your target market effortless.

PRODUCT SELECTION AND MANAGEMENT

Curating a Winning Product Catalog

Building a successful online store starts with choosing the right products. Learn how to curate a winning product catalog that aligns with your target audience and market demand.

Inventory Management Strategies for Dummies

Don't let inventory management overwhelm you. We'll introduce easy-to-understand strategies to keep track of your stock, avoid overstock or stockouts, and maintain a healthy business

Pricing Strategies Made Simple

Pricing can be a challenge for new sellers. We'll simplify pricing strategies, covering cost considerations, competitive analysis, and how to set a price that reflects the value of your products.

PRODUCT SELECTION AND MANAGEMENT: FINDING THE PERFECT FIT

To curate a winning product catalog that aligns with your target audience for an ecommerce webstore, there are several steps you can follow. These steps will help you create a catalog that resonates with your customers and drives higher engagement and conversions.

1. Understand your target audience: Gain a deep understanding of your target audience by identifying their demographics, preferences, and shopping behaviors. This will help you curate a catalog that appeals to them personally.

2. Conduct market research: Thoroughly research the market to identify trending products, popular categories, and customer demand. This will inform your product selection and keep you ahead of your competitors.

3. Gather customer insights: Reach out to your existing customers through surveys, interviews, or focus groups to understand their needs and preferences. Using this feedback, you can curate a catalog that meets their expectations.

4. Utilize data analytics: Take advantage of data analytics tools to track customer behavior on your website. This will help you understand which products are popular, which categories are performing well, and what changes you need to make to optimize your catalog.

5. Optimize product data: Ensure that your product data is accurate, comprehensive, and relevant. Include attributes and keywords that align with customer search queries to improve discoverability and increase conversions.

6. Curate visually appealing content: Use high-quality product images and compelling descriptions to showcase your products effectively. Visual content plays a crucial role in attracting and engaging customers.

7.   Organize products logically: Categorize your products in a way that makes sense to your target audience. Use simple and intuitive category names to help customers navigate your catalog easily.

8. Personalize recommendations: Implement personalized recommendation algorithms that suggest relevant products to your customers based on their browsing and purchase history. This creates a tailored experience and increases the likelihood of conversions.

9. Continuously iterate and optimize: Regularly review and update your product catalog based on customer feedback and market trends. Stay agile and adapt your catalog to meet the changing needs and preferences of your target audience.

By following these steps, you can create a winning product catalog that aligns with your target audience and drives higher engagement and conversions on your webstore, to achieve success.

Now it time to think about your inventory.

To keep track of stock and avoid overstock for a healthy business, there are several strategies you can implement. These strategies will help you maintain optimal inventory levels, prevent excess stock, and ensure that you have the right products available when customers need them.

1.   Demand forecasting: Use historical sales data, market trends, and customer insights to forecast future demand for your products. This will help you anticipate customer needs and adjust your stock levels accordingly.

2. Set minimum and maximum inventory levels: Establish minimum and maximum stock thresholds for each product. This

will help you maintain a balance between having enough stock to meet customer demand and avoiding excess inventory.

3. Use inventory management software: Invest in a reliable inventory management system that allows you to track and manage your stock levels effectively. These tools can provide real-time data on inventory levels, sales, and reordering points, making it easier to make informed decisions.

4. Implement just-in-time (JIT) inventory management: JIT is a strategy where you reorder products only when they are needed, minimizing the risk of overstocking. This can help free up capital and storage space, while ensuring efficient inventory turnover.

5. Regular inventory audits: Conduct regular audits to track and reconcile your physical inventory with your recorded stock levels. This will help identify any discrepancies and ensure accurate inventory records.

6. Supplier collaboration: Establish strong relationships with your suppliers and communicate regularly to ensure timely product deliveries. This will help prevent stockouts and delays in replenishing your inventory.

7. Analyze sales data: Continuously analyze your sales data to identify patterns and trends. This will provide insights into which products are selling well and which ones may be at risk of overstocking.

8. Monitor market and industry trends: Stay informed about market and industry trends to anticipate changes in customer demand. This will help you adjust your inventory levels and product offerings accordingly.

With these strategies, you can effectively keep track of stock, avoid overstocking, and maintain a healthy inventory for your business. Remember to regularly review and optimize your inventory management practices to ensure ongoing success and profitability.

Now my inventory is under control, what price is better to sell my product and stay ahead of my competitors?

To set a price for your products, you can implement a simple pricing strategy that aligns with your business goals and the value you provide to your customers. Here is a step-by-step guide on how to set a price for your products:

1. Understand your costs: Start by calculating your direct costs, including materials, labor, and overhead expenses. This will give you a baseline for determining your pricing.

2. Analyze the market: Conduct market research to understand the pricing landscape in your industry. Look at competitors' prices and consider factors like product differentiation, quality, and unique features. This will help you position your pricing strategy effectively.

3. Determine your pricing objectives: Decide what your pricing strategy aims to achieve. Are you focused on maximizing profits, gaining market share, or attracting price-sensitive customers? This will influence your pricing approach.

4. Choose a pricing method: There are various pricing methods you can choose from, including cost-plus pricing, competitive pricing, price skimming, penetration pricing, and value-based pricing. Each method has its advantages, so select the one that best aligns with your business goals and target market.

5. Set your price: Once you have determined your pricing

method, calculate your desired profit margin and factor in any external considerations, such as sales taxes, shipping costs, and promotional discounts. This will help you arrive at a final selling price.

6. Test and adjust: Monitor the market response to your pricing strategy and make adjustments as needed. Keep an eye on changes in costs, customer preferences, and competitor pricing to ensure your prices remain competitive and profitable.

Remember, pricing is not a one-time decision. It is an ongoing process that requires continuous evaluation and adjustment to meet market demands and achieve your business goals. By following these steps and staying informed about your industry, you'll be better equipped to set prices that reflect the value of your products and attract customers.

MARKETING AND PROMOTION FOR BEGINNERS

Crafting a Digital Marketing Plan

Digital marketing doesn't have to be complicated. We'll guide you through creating a simple and effective digital marketing plan, covering social media, email marketing, and more.

Social Media Strategies for Your Online Store

Discover beginner-friendly strategies to leverage the power of social media for your online store. From choosing the right platforms to creating engaging content, we've got you covered.

Leveraging Influencer Marketing without the Confusion

Influencer marketing can be a game-changer. Learn how to identify and collaborate with influencers relevant to your niche, even if you're just starting out.

MARKETING AND PROMOTION: AN INTRODUCTION FOR BEGINNERS

To curate a winning product catalog that aligns with your target audience for a webstore, there are several key steps you can take. By following these steps, you can ensure that your catalog is tailored to meet the needs and preferences of your customers, ultimately driving higher conversion rates and sales.

1. Understand your target audience: Start by gaining a deep understanding of your target audience. Identify their demographics, preferences, and shopping behaviors. This will help you curate a catalog that resonates with your customers on a personal level.

2. Conduct market research: Conduct thorough market research to identify trending products, popular categories, and customer demand. This will inform your product selection and help you stay ahead of your competitors.

3. Gather customer insights: Reach out to your existing customers through surveys, interviews, or focus groups to understand their needs and preferences. Their feedback can guide you in curating a catalog that aligns with their expectations.

4. Utilize data analytics: Leverage data analytics tools to track customer behavior on your website. This will help you understand which products are popular, which categories are performing well, and what changes you need to make to optimize your catalog.

5. Optimize product data: Ensure that your product data is accurate, comprehensive, and relevant. Include attributes and keywords that align with customer search queries to improve discoverability and increase conversions.

6. Curate visually appealing content: Use high-quality product images and compelling descriptions to showcase your products effectively. Visual content plays a crucial role in attracting and engaging customers.

7.   Organize products logically: Categorize your products in a way that makes sense to your target audience. Use simple and intuitive category names to help customers navigate your catalog easily.

8. Personalize recommendations: Implement personalized recommendation algorithms that suggest relevant products to your customers based on their browsing and purchase history. This creates a tailored experience and increases the likelihood of conversions.

9. Continuously iterate and optimize: Regularly review and update your product catalog based on customer feedback and market trends. Stay agile and adapt your catalog to meet the changing needs and preferences of your target audience.

By following these steps, you can create a winning product catalog that not only aligns with your target audience but also drives higher engagement and conversions on your webstore. Remember, it's important to continuously monitor and optimize your catalog to stay competitive in the ever-evolving ecommerce landscape.

How to use social media in the best way.

To leverage the power of social media for your online store, you can implement a strategy that focuses on building brand awareness, engaging with your audience, and driving traffic to your webstore. Here is a simple yet effective strategy to get you started:

1.   Choose the right social media platforms: Identify the social media platforms where your target audience is most active. This could include platforms like Facebook, Instagram, Twitter, and Pinterest. Research the demographics and user behavior of each platform to make an informed decision.

2. Define your brand's voice and tone: Develop a consistent brand voice and tone that aligns with your target audience. Decide whether you want to be playful, professional, authoritative, or informative. This will help you create content that resonates with your audience.

3. Create compelling and shareable content: Generate high-quality content that catches the attention of your audience and encourages them to share it with their networks. This can include informative blog posts, visually appealing product images, how-to videos, and customer testimonials.

4. Engage with your audience: Interact with your audience on social media by responding to comments, messages, and mentions. Show appreciation for their support and address any concerns or questions promptly. Engaging with your audience will help build trust and loyalty.

5. Run social media contests and giveaways: Organize giveaways or contests that require participants to like, comment, or share your content to enter. This will help increase your social media reach and attract new followers.

6. Collaborate with influencers: Identify influencers in your industry or niche who have a significant following on social media. Collaborate with them to promote your products or feature them in your content. Influencers can help increase your brand's visibility and credibility.

7. Utilize social media advertising: Allocate a portion of your marketing budget to social media advertising. Set up targeted ad campaigns to reach your desired audience based on demographics, interests, and behaviors. Experiment with different ad formats to determine which ones generate the best results.

8. Analyze and optimize your performance: Regularly analyze your social media performance using the insights provided by each platform. Look for patterns, trends, and opportunities for improvement. Adjust your strategy based on the data to maximize your results.

Following these simple yet effective steps, you can effectively leverage the power of social media to promote your online store, increase brand awareness, and drive traffic to your website. Remember to be consistent, authentic, and engaging with your audience to build strong relationships and achieve long-term success.

Collaborate with influencers, how to start?

To identify and collaborate with influencers in your niche, you can follow these steps:

1. Define your goals and target audience: Before seeking out influencers, it's essential to have a clear understanding of your goals and the specific audience you want to target. This will help you identify influencers who align with your brand values and niche.

2. Conduct thorough research: Use social media platforms, industry directories, and influencer marketing platforms to find influencers in your niche. Look for individuals who have a significant following, high engagement rates, and a genuine connection with their audience.

3. Evaluate influencer credibility: Analyze an influencer's content to determine if their values, style, and tone align with your brand. Look at the quality of their content, the relevancy of their posts, and the engagement they receive from their audience.

4. Engage with influencers: Before reaching out to influencers, start engaging with their content by liking, sharing, and commenting on their posts. This will help you establish a relationship and show genuine interest in their work.

5. Reach out and make a pitch: Once you've built a connection with an influencer, send them a personalized message expressing your interest in collaborating. Clearly explain the benefits of the collaboration and how it aligns with their audience's interests.

6. Negotiate and agree on terms: Discuss the details of the collaboration, such as type of content, delivery timeline, compensation, and any promotional guidelines. Be open to negotiation and ensure that both parties are comfortable with the agreed terms.

7. Track and measure results: Monitor the performance of the collaboration by tracking key metrics such as engagement rates, website traffic, and sales. This will help you evaluate the success of the collaboration and make informed decisions for future partnerships.

Remember, building strong relationships with influencers takes time and effort. It's important to approach them respectfully, engage with their content, communicate openly, and compensate them fairly. With successful collaborations, you can leverage the influence of these individuals to boost your brand's visibility and reach in your niche.

CUSTOMER SERVICE AND RETENTION

Providing Exceptional Customer Service with Ease

Good customer service is the heart of a successful online store. We'll explore practical tips to provide exceptional service and build positive relationships with your customers.

Building Customer Loyalty Programs for Dummies

Loyalty programs are a fantastic way to retain customers. We'll break down the basics of creating simple yet effective loyalty programs that keep your customers coming back.

Handling Returns and Resolving Issues Like a Pro

Returns and issues are inevitable. Learn how to handle them professionally, turning challenges into opportunities to showcase your commitment to customer satisfaction.

CUSTOMER SATISFACTION AND LOYALTY

One way to enhance customer relationships is by providing clear and detailed product descriptions. This helps set realistic expectations and reduces the likelihood of misunderstandings.

Additionally, active and genuine communication, prompt responses to inquiries, and a transparent transaction process go a long way in fostering trust and satisfaction.
Keep in mind this simple suggestions.

Listen actively and attentively to what the customer is saying. Repeat back their concerns or questions to show that you understand them.

Use polite language when communicating with customers. Avoid using slang or abbreviations that may be confusing for some people.

Be patient and empathetic towards customers who are having a difficult time. Offer support and guidance as needed.

Provide accurate information about products or services. If you don't know something, admit it and find out the answer before giving incorrect information.

Show appreciation for loyal customers by offering special discounts or rewards. This will make them feel valued and appreciated.

Follow up with customers after an interaction to ensure they had a good experience. Ask if there is anything else you can do to assist them.

Go above and beyond for customers whenever possible. This could include going out of your way to find a product or providing extra assistance without being asked.

Learn from negative experiences and use them as opportunities to improve your service. Take feedback from customers seriously and work on making changes where necessary.

Building customer loyalty programs can be a valuable strategy for keeping customers and inspiring them to come back.

Here's a step-by-step guide, simplified for easy understanding:

1. Set Clear Objectives:
Define what you want to achieve with your loyalty program, whether it's increased customer retention, higher average order value, or customer referrals.

2. Understand Your Customer Base:
Analyze your customer demographics and behavior to tailor the loyalty program to their preferences and needs.

3. Choose a Program Type:
Decide on the type of loyalty program that suits your business, such as points-based systems, tiered programs, or simple discount offers.

4. Keep it Simple:
Avoid complexity. A straightforward and easy-to-understand program is more likely to be embraced by customers.

5. Reward Meaningfully:
Offer rewards that are relevant and appealing to your customer base. This could include discounts, freebies, exclusive access, or early sales notifications.

6. Establish Clear Guidelines:
Clearly communicate how customers can earn and redeem rewards. Make the process simple and intuitive.

7. Utilize Technology:
Implement a user-friendly system, whether it's through a mobile app, website, or a physical loyalty card. Automation can

streamline the tracking and redemption process.

8. Promote Your Program:
Actively market your loyalty program through various channels, such as email, social media, and your website. Highlight the benefits of joining.

9. Track and Analyze:
Use data analytics to track the effectiveness of your loyalty program. Monitor customer participation, redemption rates, and overall program impact.

10. Seek Customer Feedback:
Regularly ask for feedback to understand how customers perceive your loyalty program. Use this information to make improvements.

11. Make it Exclusive:
Create a sense of exclusivity by offering special perks or early access to loyal customers. This makes them feel valued and appreciated.

12. Adapt and Evolve:
Be willing to adapt your loyalty program based on customer feedback and changing market conditions. Flexibility is key to long-term success.

13. Train Your Team:
Ensure your team is knowledgeable about the loyalty program and can assist customers in understanding and participating.

14. Monitor Legal Compliance:
Be aware of and comply with any legal requirements related to loyalty programs, such as data protection and consumer rights.

15. Celebrate Milestones:

Acknowledge and celebrate customer milestones within the loyalty program. This could include anniversaries, reaching a certain point threshold, or achieving a specific membership tier.

Remember, the key is to create a loyalty program that not only benefits your customers but also aligns with your business goals. Keep it simple, transparent, and focused on building a positive and lasting relationship with your customers.

Dealing with returns and issues is an integral part of any business, and handling them professionally is key to showcasing your commitment to customer satisfaction. Follow the guideline on how to turn these challenges into opportunities:

1. Timely Response:
Respond promptly to customer inquiries and issues. Acknowledge their concerns and reassure them that you are working on a resolution.

2. Empathize with the Customer:
Show empathy and understanding towards the customer's situation. Let them know that their satisfaction is your priority.

3. Clear Communication:
Communicate transparently about the steps you are taking to address the issue. Keep the customer informed throughout the process.

4. Flexible Return Policies:
Have clear and fair return policies. Make the process as seamless as possible for the customer while ensuring it aligns with your business guidelines.

5. Provide Solutions, Not Just Refunds:
Offer solutions that go beyond mere refunds, if possible. This could include exchanges, discounts on future purchases, or

additional perks as a gesture of goodwill.

6.   Learn from Feedback:
Treat every issue as a learning opportunity. Gather feedback on what went wrong and use it to improve your products or services.

7.   Personalize Your Responses:
Address customers by their names and personalize your responses. This shows that you see them as individuals, not just transactions.

8.   Apologize Sincerely:
If the issue is a result of a mistake on your end, apologize sincerely. Take responsibility and assure the customer that steps are being taken to prevent a recurrence.

9.   Train Your Customer Support Team:
Ensure your customer support team is well-trained to handle various issues. Equip them with the knowledge and skills to provide effective solutions.

10. Go the Extra Mile:
Surprise and delight customers by going the extra mile to resolve their issues. This could include expedited shipping for replacements or additional perks with their next purchase.

11. Use Positive Language:
Frame your responses in a positive and solution-oriented manner. Avoid negative language that may escalate the situation.

12. Follow Up:
After the resolution, follow up with the customer to ensure they are satisfied. This extra step demonstrates your ongoing commitment to their happiness.

13. Showcase Success Stories:

Share success stories of resolved issues (with customer consent) on your website or social media. This showcases your dedication to customer satisfaction.

14. Implement Continuous Improvement:
Regularly review your processes to identify recurring issues. Implement changes and improvements to prevent similar problems in the future.

15. Stay Calm and Professional:
Maintain a calm and professional tone, even in challenging situations. This helps in diffusing tension and creating a positive customer experience.

Remember, turning challenges into opportunities is not just about resolving the issue at hand but also about leaving a lasting positive impression on the customer. Your commitment to customer satisfaction can ultimately strengthen your brand reputation and customer loyalty.

ESSENTIAL TOOLS FOR YOUR ONLINE STORE

Choosing the Right Hosting Provider Made Simple

Don't let hosting decisions stress you out. We'll guide you through the process of selecting the right hosting provider, considering factors like speed, reliability, and customer support.

Essential E-commerce Apps and Tools Demystified

Explore must-have apps and tools that can enhance your online store's functionality. From marketing to analytics, we'll introduce tools that simplify tasks and improve efficiency.

Payment Gateways and Security Measures without the Tech Hassle

Understanding payment gateways and security is crucial. We'll break down the technical jargon, explaining how to choose secure payment gateways and implement essential security measures.

ESSENTIAL TOOLS

Selecting the right hosting provider is a crucial decision that directly impacts the performance and reliability of your online presence. Here's a guide to help you navigate through the process, with a focus on factors like speed, reliability, and customer support:

1. Evaluate Your Requirements:
Begin by understanding your website's requirements. Consider factors such as the type of website you have, expected traffic, and any specific technical needs.

2. Determine Your Budget:
Establish a realistic budget for your hosting. While cost is a factor, remember that cheaper may not always mean better when it comes to hosting services.

3. Evaluate Uptime and Reliability:
Look for a hosting provider with a strong track record of uptime. Reliability is crucial for ensuring that your website is accessible to visitors at all times.

4. Consider Server Speed:
Opt for a hosting provider that offers fast server speeds. This is essential for delivering a seamless and responsive experience to your website visitors.

5. Scalability Options:
Choose a hosting plan that allows for scalability as your website grows. This flexibility ensures that your hosting can accommodate increased traffic and resource needs.

6. Technical Support Quality:
Investigate the quality of customer support provided by the hosting company. Check for 24/7 support, response times, and the expertise of their support team.

7. Check Reviews and Testimonials:
Read reviews and testimonials from other users. This provides insights into the real-world experiences of customers with the hosting provider.

8. Understand Security Measures:
Prioritize security features offered by the hosting provider. This includes SSL certificates, regular backups, and robust security protocols to protect your website and data.

9. Investigate Data Center Locations:
Consider the geographical locations of the hosting provider's data centers. Opt for a provider with data centers closer to your target audience to improve website loading times.

10. Review Control Panel Options:
Evaluate the user-friendliness of the hosting provider's control panel. A well-designed and intuitive control panel makes it easier to manage your website and hosting settings.

11. Research Additional Features:
Look for additional features provided by the hosting company, such as one-click installations, website builders, and content delivery network (CDN) integration.

12. Understand Bandwidth and Storage Limits:
Ensure that the hosting plan you choose offers sufficient bandwidth and storage for your current and future needs. This prevents unexpected overage charges.

13. Explore Money-Back Guarantees:
Check if the hosting provider offers a money-back guarantee. This provides a safety net in case you are unsatisfied with the service within a certain period.

14. Test Their Responsiveness:
Reach out to the hosting provider's customer support with pre-sales questions. Evaluate their responsiveness and willingness to assist, which can be indicative of their ongoing support quality.

15. Seek Recommendations:
Ask for recommendations from colleagues or within online communities. Personal experiences can provide valuable insights into the performance and reliability of different hosting providers.

Remember, the right hosting provider should align with your specific needs and provide a solid foundation for your online presence. Taking the time to carefully assess these factors will contribute to a more successful and reliable hosting experience for your website.

Here are some widely regarded hosting providers known for their reliability, performance, and customer support:

Bluehost:
Why: Bluehost is a popular choice for beginners. It offers a range of hosting plans, excellent customer support, and one-click WordPress installation.

SiteGround:
Why: Known for its top-notch customer support and performance, SiteGround offers managed WordPress hosting, making it a great choice for users seeking reliability.

HostGator:
Why: HostGator provides affordable hosting plans with a user-friendly interface. They offer various hosting types, including shared, VPS, and dedicated hosting.

InMotion Hosting:

Why: InMotion Hosting is known for its reliable and fast hosting services. They offer a variety of hosting plans suitable for different business sizes.

A2 Hosting:
Why: A2 Hosting is praised for its speed and performance. They provide a range of hosting options, including shared, VPS, and dedicated hosting.

DreamHost:
Why: DreamHost is known for its commitment to open-source and offers a range of hosting plans. They also provide a generous 97-day money- back guarantee.

Kinsta:
Why: Kinsta specializes in managed WordPress hosting with a focus on performance and security. It's an excellent choice for businesses with higher budgets.

WPEngine:
Why: WPEngine is a managed WordPress hosting provider known for its speed and security features. It's suitable for businesses looking for a hassle-free WordPress hosting experience.

Hostinger:
Why: Hostinger offers budget-friendly hosting solutions without compromising on performance. They provide shared, VPS, and cloud hosting options.

Liquid Web:
Why: Liquid Web is known for its robust managed hosting solutions, including dedicated servers and cloud hosting, making it suitable for businesses with high-performance requirements.

Before making a decision, carefully consider your specific requirements, such as the type of website, expected traffic, and any specific technical needs. Additionally, read user reviews and consider factors like customer support, uptime guarantees, and scalability to ensure the hosting provider aligns with your business goals.

Improving the functionality of your online store requires using a range of applications and tools to streamline processes and boost overall efficiency.
Here's a curated list across different aspects of your online store:

1. Shopify or WooCommerce:
Purpose: E-commerce Platforms
Why: Both Shopify and WooCommerce offer user-friendly interfaces, excellent customization options, and a wide range of plugins for enhancing the functionality of your online store.

2. Mailchimp or Klaviyo:
Purpose: Email Marketing
Why: Automate email campaigns, segment your audience, and analyze customer behavior. These tools can significantly improve your marketing strategy and customer engagement.

3. Google Analytics:
Purpose: Analytics
Why: Gain insights into your website traffic, user behavior, and sales. Google Analytics provides valuable data to help you make informed decisions for optimizing your online store.

4. Canva:
Purpose: Design
Why: Create visually appealing graphics for your online store, social media, and marketing materials. Canva is user-friendly and offers templates for various design needs.

5. Oberlo or Spocket:
Purpose: Dropshipping

Why: If you engage in dropshipping, these tools integrate seamlessly with your store, allowing you to easily import and manage products from suppliers.

6. Yotpo or Trustpilot:
Purpose: Reviews and Testimonials
Why: Build trust and credibility by showcasing customer reviews. These tools help collect and display reviews on your online store.

7. Buffer or Hootsuite:
Purpose: Social Media Management
Why: Schedule posts across multiple social media platforms, analyze performance, and engage with your audience effectively.

8. Zendesk or Freshdesk:
Purpose: Customer Support
Why: Provide excellent customer support with features like ticketing, live chat, and knowledge base. These tools streamline communication and enhance customer satisfaction.

9. Hotjar or Crazy Egg:
Purpose: User Experience (UX) and Heatmaps
Why: Understand how users interact with your website through heatmaps and user recordings. Improve site usability based on actionable insights.

10. SEO Tools (e.g., SEMrush, Ahrefs):
Purpose: Search Engine Optimization
Why: Improve your online store's visibility on search engines. These tools offer keyword research, backlink analysis, and competitor insights.

11. QuickBooks or Xero:
Purpose: Accounting and Bookkeeping
Why: Simplify financial management, track expenses, and generate financial reports seamlessly.

12. PushOwl or OneSignal:
Purpose: Push Notifications
Why: Engage with customers through push notifications, promoting new products, deals, or updates.

13. LiveChat or Intercom:
Purpose: Live Chat
Why: Offer real-time support to website visitors. Improve customer satisfaction and address queries promptly.

14. Refersion or Post Affiliate Pro:
Purpose: Affiliate Marketing
Why: Establish and manage an affiliate marketing program to increase your store's reach and sales.

15. Google Workspace or Microsoft 365:
Purpose: Business Communication and Collaboration
Why: Streamline communication, collaboration, and document management with professional email, cloud storage, and collaboration tools.

Integrating these apps and tools into your online store can significantly enhance its functionality, making it more efficient and customer-friendly. Remember to regularly assess the performance of these tools and adjust your toolkit based on evolving business needs.

Understanding payment gateways and ensuring security in online transactions is paramount for the success and trustworthiness of your online store. Let's break down the technical aspects and guide you through choosing secure payment gateways and implementing essential security measures:

Choosing Secure Payment Gateways:

SSL Encryption:
Explanation: Secure Socket Layer (SSL) encryption ensures that data transmitted between the customer's browser and your website is encrypted and secure.
Implementation: Choose a payment gateway that supports SSL, and ensure your website has an SSL certificate installed.

PCI DSS Compliance:
Explanation: Payment Card Industry Data Security Standard (PCI DSS) compliance ensures that the payment gateway adheres to industry standards for handling credit card information securely.
Implementation: Verify that your chosen payment gateway is PCI DSS compliant. Most reputable gateways already adhere to these standards.

Tokenization:
Explanation: Tokenization replaces sensitive information, like credit card numbers, with unique tokens. Even if intercepted, these tokens are useless to potential attackers.
Implementation: Choose a payment gateway that employs tokenization to enhance the security of customer data.

Two-Factor Authentication (2FA):
Explanation: 2FA adds an extra layer of security by requiring users to verify their identity using two different methods.
Implementation: Enable 2FA for your admin access and any accounts associated with your payment gateway.

Fraud Detection and Prevention:
Explanation: Advanced fraud detection systems analyze transactions for patterns and anomalies, helping to prevent fraudulent activities.
Implementation: Opt for payment gateways with robust fraud prevention tools and regularly update your fraud detection parameters.

Implementing Essential Security Measures:

Regular Software Updates:
Explanation: Ensure your e-commerce platform, plugins, and any related software are regularly updated to patch vulnerabilities.
Implementation: Set up automatic updates or regularly check for updates and apply them promptly.

Data Backups:
Explanation: Regularly back up your website and customer data to minimize the impact of any potential security breaches.
Implementation: Use reliable backup solutions and schedule regular backups to an external server or cloud storage.

Secure Password Practices:
Explanation: Encourage strong, unique passwords for all accounts associated with your online store to prevent unauthorized access.
Implementation: Enforce password complexity requirements and educate your team on secure password practices.

Firewall Protection:
Explanation: Firewalls act as a barrier between your website and potential threats, filtering out malicious traffic.
Implementation: Configure a web application firewall (WAF) to protect your website from common online threats.

Employee Training:
Explanation: Educate your team about security best practices to minimize the risk of social engineering or human error.
Implementation: Conduct regular training sessions on identifying phishing attempts, password security, and overall security awareness.

Monitoring and Incident Response:
Explanation: Implement tools for continuous monitoring of your

website's security. Have an incident response plan in place to address security breaches promptly.

Implementation: Use security monitoring tools and establish a clear incident response plan for your team.

By understanding and implementing these security measures, you create a robust and secure environment for your online store. Regularly reassess your security protocols to adapt to evolving threats and technologies, ensuring a safe and trustworthy shopping experience for your customers.

Selecting the best payment gateway depends on various factors, including your business model, location, and specific requirements. Here are some widely used and trusted payment gateways known for their reliability, security, and ease of integration:

Stripe:

Why: Stripe is a versatile and developer-friendly payment gateway. It supports a wide range of payment methods, including credit cards, digital wallets, and direct bank transfers. Stripe is known for its robust security features and global reach.

PayPal:

Why: PayPal is one of the most recognized and widely used payment gateways. It supports various payment methods and is known for its ease of use. PayPal is a good choice for businesses with an international customer base.

Square:

Why: Square is known for its simplicity and is especially popular for in-person transactions. It offers a seamless online payment experience and is suitable for small to medium-sized businesses.

Authorize.Net:

Why: Authorize.Net is a well-established payment gateway with a focus on security. It provides a range of features, including recurring billing and fraud detection, making it suitable for various business types.

Braintree:
Why: Braintree, a subsidiary of PayPal, is known for its easy integration and support for various payment methods. It's a good choice for businesses looking for a smooth payment experience.

2Checkout (now Verifone):
Why: 2Checkout offers a global payment solution supporting multiple payment methods. It provides a user-friendly interface and is suitable for businesses with an international customer base.

Adyen:
Why: Adyen is a global payment platform that supports a wide range of payment methods. It's known for its scalability and is often chosen by larger enterprises with complex payment needs.

Square Online Payments:
Why: Square Online Payments is an integrated solution that works seamlessly with Square's other services. It's suitable for businesses looking for an all-in-one solution for both online and offline transactions.

Worldpay (now FIS):
Why: Worldpay is a comprehensive payment gateway that offers a range of services, including online and in-person payments. It's suitable for businesses of various sizes.

Shopify Payments:
Why: If you're using the Shopify platform, Shopify Payments is an integrated solution that simplifies the payment process. It offers competitive rates and ease of use for Shopify users.

Before choosing a payment gateway, consider factors such as transaction fees, security features, ease of integration with your e-commerce platform, and the types of payments it supports. Additionally, ensure the payment gateway complies with relevant regulations in your industry and location.

LEVERAGING TECHNOLOGY FOR SUCCESS

Integration Strategies for Dummies

Integrating different tools can streamline your operations. We'll simplify integration strategies, ensuring your tools work seamlessly together to enhance efficiency.

Scaling Your Online Store without the Headaches

Thinking about growth? Learn how to plan for scalability, ensuring your online store can handle increased traffic and sales as your business expands.

Automation Made Easy for Your E- commerce Business

Discover the power of automation. We'll explore simple automation tools and strategies that can save you time and effort, allowing you to focus on growing your business.

UTILIZING TECHNOLOGY TO ACHIEVE VICTORY.

Integrating different tools to streamline operations can indeed enhance efficiency.

Let's simplify the integration strategies :

1. Clearly Define Your Objectives:
Explanation: Begin by outlining what you aim to achieve through integration. Whether it's automating tasks, improving data accuracy, or enhancing collaboration, having a clear goal guides your integration efforts.

2. Choose User-Friendly Tools:
Explanation: Opt for tools that offer easy integration options. Look for platforms that provide intuitive interfaces and clear documentation to simplify the integration process.

3. Leverage Built-in Integrations:
Explanation: Many tools come with built-in integrations or plug-ins for popular applications. Explore and utilize these pre-built connections to save time and effort.

4. Explore API Integrations:
Explanation: APIs (Application Programming Interfaces) act as bridges between tools, enabling seamless communication. Look for tools that offer well-documented APIs, making integration smoother.

5. Prioritize Compatibility:
Explanation: Ensure that the tools you choose are compatible in terms of data formats and structures. Compatibility reduces the complexity of data mapping and transformation during integration.

6. Utilize Automation Features:

Explanation: Take advantage of automation features within the tools. Automation can streamline repetitive tasks and ensure data flows smoothly between integrated systems.

7. Start Small, Scale Gradually:
Explanation: Begin with integrating a few essential tools to test the waters. Once successful, gradually scale up the integration process to include additional tools.

8. Consider Middleware Solutions:
Explanation: Middleware platforms can act as intermediaries, simplifying communication between different tools. Look for middleware solutions that align with your integration needs.

9. Emphasize Data Security:
Explanation: Pay attention to the security features of the tools. Ensure that sensitive data is handled securely during integration by implementing encryption and authentication measures.

10. Test Thoroughly: - Explanation: Before fully implementing the integrated system, conduct thorough testing. Test for data consistency, error handling, and overall system performance to identify and address any issues.

11. Provide User Training: - Explanation: If the integration involves changes for end-users, provide adequate training. Ensuring that users are familiar with the integrated workflows promotes a smoother transition.

12. Monitor and Optimize: - Explanation: Implement monitoring tools to track the performance of integrated systems. Regularly optimize the integration based on user feedback and evolving business requirements.

13. Foster Collaboration: - Explanation: Encourage collaboration between teams involved in the integration process. Open

communication channels help address challenges more effectively.

14. Seek Vendor Support: - Explanation: If you encounter difficulties during integration, don't hesitate to seek support from the tool vendors. They often provide assistance and guidance to ensure successful integration.

15. Iterate Based on Feedback: - Explanation: Maintain a feedback loop with users and stakeholders. Gather feedback on the integrated systems' performance and iterate on the integration process based on user experiences.

By following these simplified strategies, you can seamlessly integrate different tools, enhancing efficiency and promoting a more streamlined and collaborative work environment.But let me give an example to better understand:

Scenario: Enhancing Efficiency in E-commerce Operations

Objective: Improve order processing efficiency by integrating the inventory management system, order processing tool, and customer relationship management (CRM) software.

1. Choose User-Friendly Tools:
Example: Select an inventory management system with an intuitive interface and easy integration capabilities, such as TradeGecko or Zoho Inventory.

2. Leverage Built-in Integrations:
Example: Choose an order processing tool like Shopify, which often comes with built-in integrations for popular payment gateways and shipping providers.

3. Explore API Integrations:
Example: Utilize APIs to connect the inventory management

system with the CRM software. For instance, integrate Salesforce CRM with the inventory system via APIs for seamless data exchange.

4. Prioritize Compatibility:
Example: Ensure that the order processing tool can easily communicate with the inventory system and CRM by confirming compatibility in terms of data formats and structures.

5. Utilize Automation Features:
Example: Automate the updating of inventory levels when orders are processed, ensuring real-time synchronization between the order processing tool and the inventory management system.

6. Start Small, Scale Gradually:
Example: Begin by integrating the order processing tool with the inventory system. Once successfully streamlined, gradually extend the integration to include the CRM for a holistic approach.

7. Consider Middleware Solutions:
Example: Implement middleware like Zapier to facilitate communication between the inventory system and CRM, automating tasks like updating customer records when orders are fulfilled.

8. Emphasize Data Security:
Example: Implement secure communication protocols when setting up API integrations to safeguard customer data and transaction details during order processing.

9. Test Thoroughly:
Example: Conduct thorough testing to ensure that orders placed are accurately reflected in the inventory system, and customer data is seamlessly updated in the CRM.

10. Provide User Training: - Example: Train the customer service

team on the updated workflows resulting from the integration, ensuring they can efficiently access and utilize information from the CRM during customer interactions.

11. Monitor and Optimize: - Example: Implement monitoring tools to track order processing times and inventory updates. Regularly optimize the integration based on performance metrics and user feedback.

12. Foster Collaboration: - Example: Foster collaboration between the sales team, warehouse staff, and customer service representatives to address any challenges or bottlenecks that may arise during the integrated processes.

13. Seek Vendor Support: - Example: If any technical issues arise during the integration, seek support from the vendors of the tools involved. They can provide guidance on troubleshooting and optimizing the integration.

14. Iterate Based on Feedback: - Example: Gather feedback from warehouse staff, customer service, and sales teams to identify areas for improvement. Iterate on the integration based on this feedback to continuously enhance efficiency.

By implementing these steps in this e-commerce scenario, you can seamlessly integrate the inventory management system, order processing tool, and CRM software, resulting in a more efficient and streamlined operation.

Planning for scalability is crucial to ensure that your online store can handle increased traffic and sales as your business expands. Let me explain how to do:

1. Assess Current Infrastructure:
Explanation: Begin by evaluating your current website infrastructure, including hosting, server capacity, and network

capabilities. Understand the current limitations and performance metrics.

2. Choose a Scalable Hosting Solution:
Explanation: Opt for a hosting provider that offers scalability. Consider cloud hosting services like AWS, Azure, or Google Cloud, which allow you to easily scale resources up or down based on demand.

3. Implement Content Delivery Networks (CDNs):
Explanation: Integrate a CDN to distribute static content across servers globally. This reduces latency and ensures fast loading times, particularly for users located in different geographical regions.

4. Design a Modular Architecture:
Explanation: Build a modular and flexible architecture for your website. Use microservices and containerization to enable easy scaling of specific components as needed.

5. Use Caching Mechanisms:
Explanation: Implement caching mechanisms for both static and dynamic content. This reduces server load and accelerates page loading times, contributing to a smoother user experience.

6. Employ Load Balancing:
Explanation: Introduce load balancing mechanisms to distribute incoming traffic evenly across multiple servers. This ensures that no single server bears the brunt of increased demand.

7. Optimize Database Performance:
Explanation: Optimize your database for performance. Use indexing, caching, and database sharding to distribute data efficiently and reduce database bottlenecks during peak periods.

8. Monitor Website Performance:

Explanation: Implement monitoring tools to continuously track website performance. Set up alerts for unusual spikes in traffic or any performance degradation, allowing for proactive responses.

9. Plan for Peak Traffic:
Explanation: Identify potential peak periods, such as seasonal sales or promotions. Ensure that your infrastructure can handle the increased traffic during these times without compromising performance.

10. Conduct Stress Testing:
Explanation: Regularly conduct stress tests to simulate heavy traffic conditions. This helps identify potential weaknesses in your infrastructure and allows you to address them proactively.

11. Consider Scalable E-commerce Platforms:
Explanation: If using an e-commerce platform, choose one that is inherently scalable. Platforms like Shopify Plus or Magento Enterprise are designed to handle large-scale operations.

12. Automate Scalability Responses:
Explanation: Implement automated scaling responses. Configure your infrastructure to scale resources automatically in response to increasing demand, ensuring a seamless and instantaneous adjustment.

13. Future-Proof Technology Choices:
Explanation: Choose technologies and frameworks that are adaptable to future advancements. This helps future-proof your website and ensures compatibility with emerging scalability solutions.

14. Collaborate with Scalability Experts:
Explanation: Collaborate with scalability experts or consultants to assess your infrastructure and provide tailored recommendations for scalability improvements.

15. Regularly Review and Update:
Explanation: Scalability is an ongoing process. Regularly review your scalability plan, update infrastructure as needed, and stay informed about the latest technologies to keep your online store at its peak.

By following these steps, you'll be well-prepared to scale your online store effectively, accommodating increased traffic and sales as your business expands. This strategic approach ensures a seamless and responsive experience for your customers even during periods of heightened demand.

Leveraging automation tools and strategies can significantly save time and effort, freeing you to concentrate on business growth. Here's a guide to simple automation tools and strategies:

1. Email Marketing Automation:
Tool: Mailchimp, Sendinblue, or HubSpot
Explanation: Use email marketing platforms to automate your email campaigns, from welcome emails to personalized newsletters. Set up triggers based on customer behavior to nurture leads and drive engagement.

2. Social Media Scheduling:
Tool: Buffer, Hootsuite, or Later
Explanation: Schedule your social media posts in advance. Plan your content calendar, and these tools will automatically publish posts across various platforms at optimal times, saving you the hassle of manual posting.

3. Customer Relationship Management (CRM): Tool: Salesforce, Zoho CRM, or HubSpot CRM
Explanation: Implement a CRM system to automate customer interactions, track leads, and manage sales processes. Set up automated follow-up emails and reminders to ensure no potential

opportunity falls through the cracks.

4.   E-commerce Order Processing:
Tool: Shopify, WooCommerce, or Magento
Explanation: If you run an online store, use e-commerce platforms that automate order processing tasks. This includes inventory management, order fulfillment, and even sending order confirmation emails.

5. Task and Project Management: Tool: Asana, Trello, or Monday.com
Explanation: Streamline your task management by automating repetitive workflows. Set up recurring tasks, assign responsibilities automatically, and track project progress effortlessly.

6.   Chatbot for Customer Support:
Tool: Drift, Intercom, or Chatbot.com
Explanation: Integrate chatbots on your website to handle common customer queries. This saves time by providing instant responses and directing users to relevant resources, reducing the need for manual support.

7. Invoicing and Payment Reminders: Tool: QuickBooks, FreshBooks, or Wave
Explanation: Automate your invoicing process and set up payment reminders. These tools can send invoices automatically and alert you when payments are due or overdue, improving cash flow management.

8.   Social Media Analytics:
Tool: Google Analytics, Facebook Insights, or Twitter Analytics
Explanation: Automate the gathering of social media analytics data. Set up regular reports to track the performance of your social media campaigns without manual data collection.

9. Data Backups:
Tool: Dropbox, Google Drive, or Backblaze
Explanation: Automate data backups to the cloud. This ensures that your essential business files are regularly and securely backed up, reducing the risk of data loss.

10. Employee Onboarding:
Tool: BambooHR, Workday, or Gusto
Explanation: Simplify employee onboarding by automating paperwork, documentation, and training processes. This ensures a smoother and more consistent onboarding experience for new hires.

11. Email Filtering and Organization:
Tool: Gmail Filters, Outlook Rules, or SaneBox
Explanation: Set up rules and filters in your email client to automatically categorize and prioritize emails. This helps you focus on crucial communications and reduces time spent on sorting through your inbox.

12. Content Publishing Automation:
Tool: WordPress (with plugins like Jetpack), Medium, or Buffer
Explanation: Schedule and automate content publishing. Write blog posts in advance and set them to publish automatically at specified times, maintaining a consistent content schedule.

13. Appointment Scheduling:
Tool: Calendly, Acuity Scheduling, or Doodle
Explanation: Allow clients or team members to schedule appointments without the back-and-forth. These tools automate appointment booking, saving time and avoiding scheduling conflicts
.

14. Expense Tracking:
Tool: Expensify, Receipts by Wave, or QuickBooks
Explanation: Automate expense tracking by syncing your

business accounts. Capture and categorize receipts automatically, making financial record-keeping more efficient.

15. SEO Monitoring:
Tool: SEMrush, Moz, or Ahrefs
Explanation: Automate SEO monitoring to track your website's performance. Receive regular reports on keyword rankings, backlinks, and site health, allowing you to make data-driven decisions for optimization.

By incorporating these simple automation tools and strategies into your business processes, you'll save valuable time and resources. This, in turn, enables you to focus on strategic aspects of growing your business, fostering efficiency and productivity.

CONCLUSION

Summary of Key Takeaways

Congratulations on completing the journey through "E-commerce Success: The Ultimate Beginner's Guide"! Let's recap the key takeaways from each section:

Getting Started: Understand the basics of e-commerce and set realistic goals.

Market Research: Demystify market research and identify your target audience.

Online Presence: Choose a domain, design a user-friendly website, and select the right platform.

Starting and Running Your Store: List products, handle payments, and ensure efficient order fulfillment.

Product Selection and Management: Curate a winning product catalog, manage inventory, and set the right prices.

Marketing and Promotion: Craft a digital marketing plan, use social media effectively, and explore influencer marketing.

Customer Service and Retention: Provide exceptional service, create loyalty programs, and handle returns professionally.

Essential Tools: Choose the right hosting provider, explore

essential e-commerce tools, and ensure payment security.

Leveraging Technology: Integrate tools effectively, plan for scalability, and leverage automation.

CONCLUSION

Your Next Steps on the E-commerce Journey

Starting an e-commerce business can be an exciting journey, but it can also be overwhelming. To help you navigate through the process, here are some steps to keep in mind.

Firstly, it's important to implement what you've learned. This means applying the knowledge you've gained from various resources to your online store. Whether it's optimizing your website for search engines or improving your customer service, make sure to put your newfound knowledge into practice.

Secondly, stay curious. The e-commerce landscape is constantly evolving, and it's important to stay up-to-date with the latest strategies and technologies. This could mean attending industry events, reading industry blogs or joining online forums to stay informed.

Thirdly, connect with the community. Building relationships with other e- commerce business owners can be an invaluable resource. Joining a community of like-minded individuals can provide you with ongoing support, discussions, and shared experiences that can help you grow your business.

Lastly, explore additional resources. There are countless resources available to help you enhance your understanding of e-commerce. From podcasts to webinars, make sure to check out the provided links for additional resources that can further enhance your knowledge.

In conclusion, embarking on your e-commerce journey can be a fulfilling experience, but it's important to keep these steps in mind. By implementing what you've learned, staying curious, connecting with the community and exploring additional resources, you can set yourself up for success in the ever-changing world of e-commerce.

Embarking on the road to success in your online selling venture is quite the exciting journey! It's like navigating through a bustling marketplace where each interaction and listing is a step forward in achieving your goals. Picture it as curating a vibrant display of your used treasures, each one telling a unique story.

To really make a mark, think of your product listings as little narratives. Craft descriptions that not only highlight the features but also convey the character of the item. It's like introducing a friend to a potential buyer, making the connection more personal and inviting.

Navigating the online landscape can be a bit like exploring a new city. Try different neighborhoods (platforms) to see where your offerings resonate the most. Just like in a community, being responsive to questions and feedback is key. It's the online equivalent of chatting with customers face- to-face, building that trust that keeps them coming back.

Now, about the tech side of things – don't sweat it too much! Think of it as learning the local language. Sure, it might be a bit challenging at first, but there are user-friendly platforms out there that act like a friendly local guide, helping you navigate without getting lost in the technical jargon.

Remember, this journey is all about growth and adaptability.

Just like a market evolves with new trends, stay tuned to what's happening in the online selling world. Embrace change, try new approaches, and enjoy the adventure!

I want to express my sincere gratitude for choosing to be a part of our community of satisfied customers. It brings me great joy to know that you've found something special among our offerings, and I truly appreciate your trust in our service.

Your decision to make a purchase not only supports our small business but also adds another layer to the unique stories embedded in each item we share. I'm confident that the [product name] you've chosen will bring you as much happiness and utility as it did for its previous owner.

In this journey of online selling, the connections we make with customers like you are invaluable. Your satisfaction is our ultimate goal, and it fuels our passion to continually offer quality items and a seamless shopping experience.

If you ever have questions, feedback, or just want to share your experience with our community, please feel free to reach out. We're here to ensure your journey with us is nothing short of delightful.

Thank you once again for being a part of our story. May this book serve you well and bring a touch of joy to your life.

ABOUT THE AUTHOR

Steve M

Steve M Styla DIgital Founder

Meet Steve M, a seasoned entrepreneur with over 12 years of hands-on experience in the dynamic world of online selling. Steve has successfully navigated the e-commerce landscape, building a track record of success that includes a remarkable history on platforms like eBay.

Experience and Expertise

With a career spanning more than a decade, Steve has honed his skills in every aspect of online retail. From strategic product selection to effective marketing and customer service, he's been there and done that. Steve's journey started with a passion for connecting buyers with quality products, and over the years, he has evolved into a trusted authority in the

e-commerce space. Success Story on eBay

Steve's achievements aren't just theoretical; they're backed by a tangible success story. His ventures on eBay stand as a testament to his ability to understand market trends, connect with customers, and build thriving online

stores. Whether it's sourcing in-demand products or mastering the art of customer satisfaction, Steve's success on eBay showcases the practical insights he brings to the table.

Dedicated Mentorship

Beyond personal success, Steve is passionate about sharing his knowledge with aspiring entrepreneurs. He believes in demystifying the complexities of online selling, making it accessible to everyone. Steve's dedication to mentorship extends beyond this ebook, as he actively engages with the e-commerce community to provide guidance, answer questions, and foster a supportive learning environment.

Get ready to embark on a journey of e-commerce success with Steve M — your experienced guide who combines years of practical experience with a genuine commitment to helping you achieve your online selling goals

www.ingramcontent.com/pod-product-compliance
Lightning Source LLC
Chambersburg PA
CBHW062243290526
45794CB00006B/2384